C000133904

日本料理 Japanese Cuisine
for Beginners

Laure Kié

Photographs: Patrice Hauser

h.f.ullmann

目次 # Contents

いらっしゃいませ
Irasshaimase !*

* Welcome!

Laure Kié 己絵

Born in Tokyo to a Japanese mother and French father, Laure Kié grew up with Japanese family cooking. Frequent trips to Japan immersed her in the richness of Japanese culinary heritage, allowing her to develop a flair for a natural, simple cuisine, bursting with flavor, which she passes on in her cookery courses today.

Japanese cuisine

Healthy, varied, balanced, and esthetically pleasing—the virtues of traditional Japanese cuisine speak for themselves… Above all, it is surprisingly delicious! While extremely varied, Japanese cuisine is based on a few key recipes that are important to master. These recipes are the result of thousands of years of tradition—a veritable treasure trove of culinary delights, combining flavors, nutrition, and estheticism. Let me share with you these essential recipes from a culinary tradition that is unique and elegant, yet so easy to reproduce every day.

Mortar
(suribashi)

Rice bowl

Rolling mat (maki

調理器具
Equipment

Wooden drop-lid

General-purpos
kni

Daikon grater

Bamboo strainer
(zaru)

Rice paddle

Vegetable
knife

Kitchen chopsticks

Fish filleting knife

Square skillet
(tamagoyaki)

Japanese mandoline

材料 # Ingredients

In order to make the recipes in this book, some basic ingredients are essential, such as soy sauce, mirin, rice vinegar, sesame oil, miso, and seaweed—substitutions will not do! These ingredients are readily available from stores selling organic produce (which usually stock a good range of Japanese products), from Asian grocers, or even from supermarkets. For most of the other ingredients, I will also list suitable alternatives throughout this book.

Nori

Seaweed sheets suitable for sushi

Soy sauce

Rice vinegar

Mirin

Sweetened rice alcohol

Kinako

Toasted soy flour

Toasted sesame oil

Potato flour

Sake

Wakame

Seaweed suitable for soups and salads

Udon

hick wheat flour noodles

Rice

Ramen

Chinese wheat flour noodles

Kombu

aweed suitable for broths

Somen

Thin wheat flour noodles

Soba

Buckwheat flour noodles

Tofu

Azuki beans

Red beans

Sesame seeds

Hijiki
Seaweed suitable for simmering

Miso
Fermented soybean paste

Umeboshi
Pickled plums

Sesame paste

Agar
Gelatin-like seaweed

Matcha
Green powdered tea

Ginger

Preserved ginger

Wasabi
Japanese mustard

Shiitake

Golden oak mushrooms

Scallions

Bok choy

Chinese cabbage

Kaki

Daikon

Japanese radish

Katsuobushi

Dried bonito shavings

Shiso

Perilla leaves

Bean sprouts

調理の基本

Basic recipes

Mastering these basic recipes is the key to success. In Japan, one judges a good cook by the quality of his or her dashi, the Japanese broth. Here you will find the essential techniques required to make the celebrated dashi, Japanese rice, miso soup, and the flavorful teriyaki sauce!

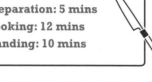

Preparation: 5 mins
Cooking: 12 mins
Standing: 10 mins

Serves 4

- 2¼ cups (450 g) white rice (Japanese rice or short-grain Italian risotto rice)
- 2½ cups (600 ml) water

Japanese rice

Rinse the rice. Repeat several times until the water runs clear.

Drain and place in a large saucepan with the water.

Cover, bring to a boil, then cook for 12 minutes over very low heat.

Remove the saucepan from the heat and allow to stand for about 10 minutes with the lid on.

In Japanese the word rice (gohan - ご飯) also means meal, which underlines the importance of this cereal grain in Japanese cooking. Japanese (Japonica) rice is a short-grain variety with a high starch content, which gives it a slightly sticky feel. I frequently substitute short-grain Italian risotto rice, available in organic stores. All Japanese families have a rice cooker, but the method of cooking it in a saucepan described in this recipe will enable you to achieve rice of a good consistency, soft yet firm to the bite.

Variation: Takikomi gohan

Rinse the rice and place it in the saucepan as described in the recipe above.

Add 3 tablespoons of soy sauce, 3 tablespoons of mirin, 1 piece of kombu, 2 inches (5 cm) long, and 1 dried shiitake mushroom to the saucepan.

Pour on the water and cook as described in the previous recipe. This will yield a very flavorful rice.

Tip
If you have time, let the rice stand for 30 minutes in the water before you cook it; this will enable the grains to swell and moisten and your rice will be all the better for it.

Preparation: 5 mins
Cooking: 2 mins

- 3 tbsp (40 g) superfine sugar
- 1 tsp salt
- ⅓ cup (75 ml) rice vinegar
- 4 servings cooked rice (see quantities and preparation instructions on page 16)

Sushi rice

Dissolve the sugar and salt in the vinegar in a saucepan over low heat (taking care not to allow the mixture to boil.)

Place the cooked rice in a bowl. Stir the vinegar mixture through the rice carefully so as not to crush the grains (cool the rice with a fan if possible); in this way, the rice will have a good shine to it.

Cover the rice with a damp cloth, to avoid it drying out, and allow to stand until you are ready to serve.

Tip
For a fruitier flavor, you can substitute raspberry or cider vinegar for the rice vinegar.

Preparation: 2 mins
Standing: 2 hours
Cooking: 3 mins

- Dried kombu, 2 in (5 cm)
- 1 dried shiitake mushroom
- 1 quart (1 liter) cold water

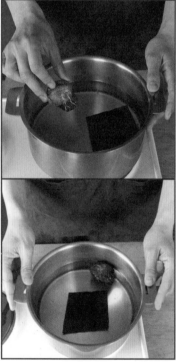

Dashi broth

Put all the ingredients in a saucepan and allow to stand at room temperature for at least 2 hours.

Place the saucepan over low heat and warm through. Turn off the heat just before the mixture comes to a boil and allow to cool. Strain the broth.

Dashi broth is the staple of Japanese cookery. It forms the basis of many dishes such as the famous miso soup, but it is also used in sauces or for cooking vegetables, fish, or meat. Dashi can be made with kombu seaweed, dried bonito shavings (katsuobushi), dried shiitake mushroom, or dried sardine (niboshi).

Tip
For maximum flavor, steep the kombu and the shiitake mushroom in the water overnight.

Makes 1 quart (1 liter)

- 1 handful katsuo (dried bonito shavings)
- 1 quart (1 liter) cold water

Variation: Dashi broth with katsuo

Pour the water into a saucepan, add the dried bonito shavings, and allow to stand at room temperature for at least 2 hours.

Place the saucepan over low heat. Turn off the heat just before the mixture comes to a boil and allow to cool. Strain the broth.

Katsuo bushi is cooked bonito (fish), which is dried then flaked into shavings. It is used mainly as the basis for dashi broth, but it can also be a condiment for vegetables or rice, often served with soy sauce.

 Tip
You can combine the two variations on dashi broth by using all **3** ingredients (bonito shavings, shiitake mushroom, and kombu).

Serves 4

- 3⅓ cups (800 ml) dashi broth (see p. 20)
- scant 4 tbsp miso paste
- 1 tbsp dried wakame
- ½ tbsp sesame seeds (optional)

Miso soup

Bring the dashi broth to a boil in a saucepan. Add the wakame seaweed then take the saucepan off the heat.

Dilute the miso paste in a little broth to moisten it slightly.

Stir this mixture into the saucepan. Add a few sesame seeds if using.

You can liven up your miso soup with an extra ingredient (tofu, mushrooms, leeks, carrots, onions…)—cook your chosen ingredient in the broth before you add the miso.

Tip
Do not boil the miso paste or it will lose its nutritional qualities and its flavor. Add it at the last minute.

Seasonings

Here are a few indispensable sauces to go with meat or vegetable skewers, noodles, salads, fritters, fondues…

Ponzu sauce

Goma-dare

Yakitori sauce

Miso sauce

Tonkatsu sauce

Tsuyu (tempura sauce)

Teriyaki sauce

Ume sauce

Goma-dare

Makes 1 cup (250 ml)

- ½ cup (120 g) sesame paste (tahini)
- ½ cup (120 ml) dashi broth (see p. 20) or soy milk
- 2 tbsp rice vinegar
- 4 tbsp soy sauce

In a bowl, dilute the tahini in a quarter of the broth. Gradually add the remaining broth to the bowl, stirring continuously, as if making mayonnaise.

Add the soy sauce and rice vinegar. Mix to obtain a smooth sauce.

Store this sauce in a jar in the refrigerator for up to 2 weeks.

Miso sauce

Makes ⅔ cup (150 ml)

- scant 2 tbsp (30 g) miso paste
- 2 tbsp dashi broth (see p. 20) or cold water
- 1 tbsp mirin
- 1 tbsp sesame paste (tahini)

Mix the miso paste with the remaining ingredients in a bowl.

Strain the mixture.

Can be stored in a jar in the refrigerator for up to 2 weeks.

Ponzu sauce

Makes 1 cup (250 ml)

- 1 small handful dried bonito shavings (or 1 dried shiitake mushroom)
- dried kombu, 2 in (5 cm) piece
- 4 tbsp lemon juice
- 4 tbsp tangerine juice
- 4 tbsp mirin
- ½ cup (120 ml) soy sauce

The day before, place the dried bonito shavings and kombu seaweed in a jar and cover with soy sauce. Close the jar, and allow to infuse overnight in the refrigerator.

On the day you wish to serve it, strain the sauce then add the remaining ingredients.

Can be stored in the refrigerator for up to 2 weeks.

Yakitori sauce

Makes generous ¾ cup (200ml)

- ½ cup (120 ml) sake
- 5 tbsp mirin
- ½ tsp powdered chicken bouillon (or 1 chicken bouillon cube)
- ⅔ cup (150 ml) soy sauce
- 3 tbsp superfine sugar

Place all the ingredients in a large saucepan. Bring to a boil, stirring continuously to dissolve the sugar and the bouillon, then simmer over low heat for about 15 minutes until you obtain a syrupy consistency.

Can be stored in the refrigerator for up to 2 weeks.

Tonkatsu sauce

Makes generous ³/₄ cup (200 ml)

- 4 tbsp apple sauce
- 1 tbsp fresh ginger, grated
- 1 clove garlic, finely chopped
- 4 tbsp mirin
- 4 tbsp tomato paste
- 1 tbsp rice vinegar
- 2 tbsp soy sauce
- 4 tbsp superfine sugar

Place all the ingredients in a large saucepan. Bring to a boil, stirring continuously to dissolve the sugar, then allow to simmer over low heat for about 5 minutes until syrupy.

Can be stored in the refrigerator for up to 2 weeks.

Teriyaki sauce

Makes 1¹/₄ cups (300 ml)

- generous ³/₄ cup (200 ml) soy sauce
- ²/₃ cup (150 ml) mirin
- 4 tbsp superfine sugar

Place all the ingredients in a saucepan. Bring to a boil then lower the heat and let the sauce reduce for 5 minutes, stirring occasionally.

Can be stored in the refrigerator for up to 2 weeks.

Tsuyu (tempura sauce)

Makes 1¹/₄ cups (300 ml)

- 1 small handful dried bonito shavings
- 6 tbsp mirin
- 6 tbsp soy sauce
- generous ¾ cup (200 ml) cold water

Pour the water into a saucepan then add the remaining ingredients. Heat the mixture over a medium heat until it comes to a boil. Take off the heat and allow to cool.

Strain the sauce.

Can be stored in the refrigerator for up to 1 week.

Ume sauce

Makes ¹/₃ cup (90 ml)

- 2 tbsp umeboshi paste
- 2 tbsp sake
- 2 tbsp mirin

Mix all the ingredients in a bowl.

Can be stored in the refrigerator for up to 3 weeks.

Soups and salads

サラダと汁物

In Japan, a meal always includes soup, which is most often based on miso, a fermented soybean paste renowned for its many nutritional qualities. Indeed, miso soup is one of the essential dishes served in a traditional Japanese breakfast.

Preparation: 15 mins
Cooking: 15 mins

- 1 small carrot, peeled
- ½ sweet potato, peeled
- ½ daikon, peeled
- 1 leek
- scant 4 tbsp miso paste
- 3⅓ cups (800 ml) dashi broth (see p. 20)
- 1 tbsp toasted sesame oil
- 3½ oz (100 g) firm tofu
- 2 thin slices unsalted pork belly, shredded
- 1 tbsp soy sauce
- ½ scallion, thinly sliced

Kenchin soup

Slice the carrot, sweet potato, and daikon into thin rounds; cut these into two or four, depending on their size.

Slice the leek into rounds.

In a bowl, dilute the miso paste in a little broth.

Heat the oil in a large saucepan and fry the vegetables, tofu, and pork belly over high heat for 3–4 minutes. Pour over the remaining broth and allow to simmer over medium heat for about 10 minutes, until the vegetables are tender.

Using your fingers, break up the tofu into large chunks. Add these to the saucepan and cook for a further 5 minutes.

Add the soy sauce and the diluted miso paste to the saucepan.

Divide the hot soup between bowls and garnish with the thinly sliced scallion.

Preparation: 10 mins
Standing: 10 mins
Cooking: 10 mins

- 14 oz (400 g) clams
- 2 tbsp dried wakame
- 4 tbsp white miso paste
- 1 tbsp chopped scallion

Miso-flavored clam soup

Rinse the clams, then soak them in a large quantity of cold water for about 10 minutes.

Rehydrate the wakame seaweed in a bowl of water for 10 minutes. Drain and use your hands to squeeze out excess water.

Bring 3⅓ cups (800 ml) cold water to a boil in a saucepan. Plunge the clams into the saucepan of boiling water and cook over high heat for 4–5 minutes, until they open. Lower the heat.

In a small bowl, dilute the miso paste with a little cooking water from the clams. Add the diluted paste to the saucepan (taking care not to let it boil.)

Divide the wakame and the clams between 4 bowls. Pour over the miso broth and sprinkle with chopped scallion. Serve immediately.

Very high in mineral content, wakame is one of the seaweeds most frequently used in Japanese cooking. It is one of the key ingredients in miso soup, and is found in most salads. It is usually available in dried form (to be rehydrated) but it can be also be bought fresh in organic stores.

Tip
You can use cockles instead of clams.

Preparation: 12 mins
Standing: 10 mins
Cooking: 8 mins

- 9 oz (250 g) soba noodles
- 4½ oz (125 g) crabmeat
- ½ cup (100 g) daikon, grated
- 4 tbsp dried wakame
- 8 tbsp ponzu sauce (see p. 26)
- grated lime zest to garnish (optional)

Soba noodle salad with crab

Rehydrate the dried wakame seaweed in a bowl of cold water for 10 minutes. Drain and use your hands to squeeze out excess water.

Cook the soba noodles in a large saucepan of boiling water according to the instructions on the packet (about 5 minutes.)

Rinse the noodles under cold running water and drain them.

Pile up the noodles on a serving platter. Add the wakame and the crabmeat, then sprinkle with ponzu sauce. Garnish with grated daikon and lime zest.

Buckwheat is used in France to make the famous Breton buckwheat pancakes. In Japan, however, this cereal is used exclusively to make noodles. Indeed, in Japanese, soba means buckwheat.

Cucumber and wakame seaweed salad

Serves 4

Preparation: 10 mins
Standing: 10 mins
No cooking

- ½ cucumber
- 2 tbsp dried wakame
- 1 tbsp rice vinegar
- ½ tbsp sesame seeds
- 1 tbsp soy sauce
- 1 tbsp toasted sesame oil
- pinch of salt

Rehydrate the dried wakame in a bowl of cold water for 10 minutes.

Meanwhile, peel the cucumber, cut in half lengthways, de-seed, and slice thinly. Place in a strainer with the salt for about 10 minutes and leave to drain.

Drain the wakame and use your hands to squeeze out the excess water.

In a salad bowl, mix the cucumber and the wakame with the remaining ingredients.

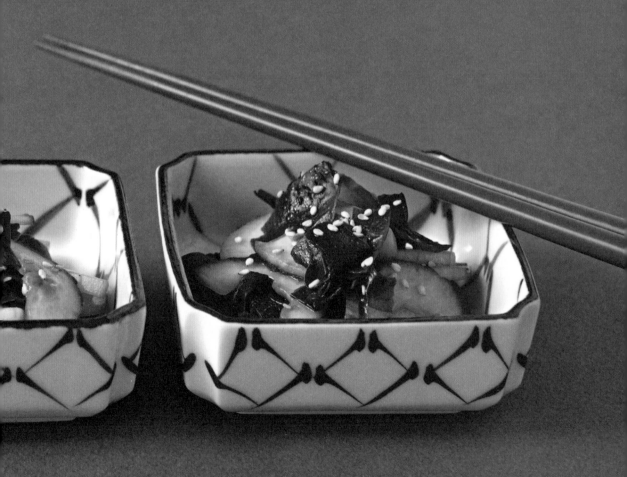

Radish salad with sprouted seeds

Preparation: 8 mins
No cooking

Wash and spin the salad leaves.

Wash and trim the radishes; cut them into thin rounds.

Arrange the salad leaves on a serving plate, sprinkle with the radish rounds, and garnish with sprouted seeds.

In a bowl, mix the sesame oil, soy sauce, and the lemon juice until emulsified. Add the garlic.

Pour the dressing over the salad just before serving.

- 1½ cups (120 g) mixed salad leaves
- 8 small radishes
- 1 handful sprouted seeds
- ½ clove garlic, finely chopped
- 1 tbsp lemon juice
- 1½ tbsp soy sauce
- 3 tbsp toasted sesame oil

Serves 4

Tip
Use toasted sesame oil—not plain sesame oil—for all the recipes in this book. It has a much stronger flavor.

米と麺

Rice and noodles

Japanese people do not eat bread, but they have rice at every meal... even breakfast! It is most often served plain, in a bowl, as an accompaniment to other dishes; it can, however, constitute the sole element in a meal: for example, onigiri, those small Japanese-style sandwiches that can be enjoyed at any time of day. And, if no rice is on the menu, inevitably there will be noodles instead!

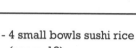

**Preparation: 30 mins
No cooking**

Serves 4 (Makes 24)

- 4 small bowls sushi rice
  (see p. 18)
- 4 slices tamagoyaki (without
  spinach: see p. 118)
- 8 slices (or steaks) extra-
  fresh salmon
- 4 slices extra-fresh
  sea bream
- 4 large cooked shrimp
- 4 fillets fresh anchovy
- 1 scallion, finely chopped
- 1 tsp fresh ginger, grated
- ¼ cup salmon roe
- 1 sheet nori
- wasabi

Sushi

Salmon sushi

Skin and bone the salmon (taking care to remove all
the dark parts sticking to the flesh.)

Cut the salmon into ¼ in- (½ cm-) thick slices.

Dampen your hands to avoid the rice sticking.

Place a small quantity of sushi rice in the palm of
your hand. Press down lightly on the rice and roll it
into a small oval (or sausage) shape (the base should
be flatter.)

Using your finger, smear a small amount of wasabi
on top of the rice or in the center of the salmon slice.

Lay the salmon slice (wasabi side down) on top of
the rice.

Using 2 fingers, press down firmly on the fish so
it adheres to the rice. Arrange the sushi on a
serving plate.

To serve
- Soy sauce
- Pickled ginger

Sea bream sushi

Make 1 rice oval shape (see opposite, steps 3 and 4.) Skin and bone the sea bream. Cut into ¼ in- (½ cm-) slices (to obtain sufficiently large slices, cut into the fillet almost parallel to the rolling mat, not vertically.)

Proceed as for salmon sushi (see steps 5, 6, and 7) then garnish with chopped scallion.

Anchovy sushi

Make 1 rice oval shape (see opposite, steps 3 and 4.) Proceed as for salmon sushi (see steps 5, 6, and 7) then garnish with grated fresh ginger.

Serve the sushi with pickled ginger, dipping them in a little soy sauce.

Sushi (continued)

Sushi with salmon roe

Make 1 rice oval shape (see p. 42, steps 3 and 4.) Cut 1 strip of nori wider than the height of the rice ball. Wrap the seaweed strip round the rice.

Use a small spoon to place the salmon roe on top of the rice.

Shrimp sushi

Make 1 rice oval shape (see p. 42, steps 3 and 4.) Peel 1 shrimp, leaving the tail on. Cut open from the stomach to the back without cutting the shrimp in two.

Proceed as for salmon sushi (see p. 42, steps 5, 6, and 7.)

Tamagoyaki sushi

Make 1 oval rice shape (see p. 42, steps 3 and 4.) Cut 1 thin strip of nori seaweed. Stick the omelet slice on the rice as for the salmon. Wrap the seaweed strip round the rice.

Serves 4 (2 large maki + 4 thinner maki)

Preparation: 35 mins
No cooking

- 4 small bowls sushi rice
  (see recipe on p. 18)
- 4 sheets nori
- wasabi and soy sauce

For the futo-maki
- 3 oz (80 g) very fresh
  salmon, cut into strips
- ¼ peeled cucumber,
  de-seeded and cut into
  small thick batons
- ¼ tamagoyaki (without the
  spinach: see p. 118), cut into
  small lengths
- 1 handful arugula

For the hosso-maki
- ½ avocado, cut into strips
- 2 tbsp black sesame seeds
- 1 handful arugula
- 1 handful sprouted seeds

Maki

Futo-maki (Makes 2 large rolls = 16 bite-size pieces)

Place 1 sheet of nori seaweed on a rolling mat, with the shiny, smooth side against the mat.

Spread a layer of rice over three quarters of the nori seaweed. Arrange half the ingredients in a single layer on top of the rice.

Keeping the filling ingredients in place with your fingers, lift up the edge of the mat closest to you.

Roll the nori so the filling ingredients are enveloped in the rice: the edge of the seaweed sheet that is closest to you must touch the outer edge of the rice strip. Using the mat, press down with your hands so as to form a cylinder.

Slowly roll up the maki, steadily pulling the mat with one hand all the while.

Each time you roll, press down on the mat so the nori sheet adheres well.

Make a second maki in the same way.

Tip
The nori sheet must not be dampened, otherwise it would become too elastic.

Remove the mat and place the rolled up maki on a cutting board.

Using a sharp knife, cut the maki in two.

Cut each half in two once again.

Between cuttings, moisten the blade of your knife with a damp cloth to avoid the rice grains sticking to the blade.

Cut the sections once again to obtain 8 bite-size pieces.

Hosso-maki (Makes 4 small rolls = 24 bite-size pieces)

Cut the nori seaweed sheet in two.

Lay ½ nori sheet on the rolling mat, with the shiny, smooth side against the mat.

Spread out a layer of rice on three quarters of the nori seaweed. Arrange a quarter of the ingredients in a single layer on top of the rice. Proceed as for futo-maki, but cutting the sushi into 6 bite-size pieces instead of 8.

Make 3 further maki in the same way.

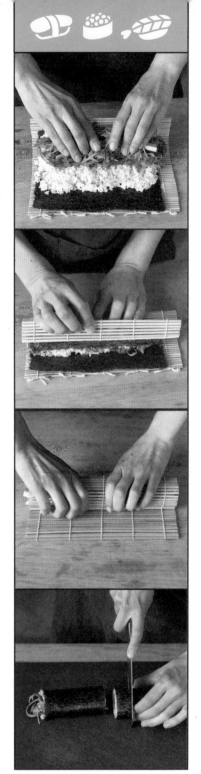

Sushi

Maki

Udon noodles with chicken dango meatballs

Preparation: 20 mins
Cooking: 25 mins

Serves 4

For the chicken dango meatballs
- 7 oz (200 g) chicken breast, minced
- 1½ tbsp potato flour
- 1 egg yolk
- 2 tbsp fresh ginger, grated
- 1 clove garlic, crushed
- 8 sprigs cilantro, finely chopped
- 1 tbsp soy sauce

To garnish
- 14 oz (400 g) udon noodles
- 2 quarts (2 liters) dashi broth (see p. 20)
- 4 tbsp soy sauce
- 2 tbsp mirin
- 4 shiitake mushrooms (or button mushrooms)
- 1 carrot, peeled and chopped
- 1 leek, chopped
- ¼ Chinese cabbage, shredded
- generous ½ cup (100 g) fresh spinach

First make the chicken meatballs: mix all the ingredients in a large bowl until you have a homogeneous mixture. Set aside.

Cook the noodles in a large saucepan of boiling water according to the instructions on the packet (3–5 minutes.) Rinse the noodles under cold running water and drain them.

Bring the dashi broth, soy sauce, and mirin to a boil in a large saucepan.

Remove the stalk from the shiitake mushrooms and add them to the saucepan with the carrot and leek. Lower the heat and simmer for 10 minutes.

Add the Chinese cabbage. Using two tablespoons, form meatballs with the chicken mixture then add them gradually to the saucepan. Cook for 4–5 minutes (they should bob up to the surface.)

Add the spinach and cook for a few minutes until wilted.

Divide the noodles among 4 large bowls. Add the chicken meatballs and the garnish. Pour over the broth to cover and serve immediately.

Tip
You can prepare and cook the meatballs and the garnish the day before. The broth will taste even better.

Udon noodles with chicken dango meatballs

Yakisoba

Cut the pork belly slices into strips.

Thinly slice the cabbage and onion.

Heat the oil in a wok and stir-fry the onion and ginger for 2 minutes, stirring continuously. Add the cabbage and pork belly and cook for a further 4–5 minutes, stirring continuously.

Add the noodles and ½ cup (120 ml) water. Stir-fry them for 2 minutes then mix in the oyster and soy sauces, coating all the ingredients well.

Divide the mixture between plates. Garnish with pickled ginger and strips of nori seaweed just before serving.

Even if their name is made up of the word "soba", yakisoba noodles are not made with buckwheat, but with ordinary wheat. They can easily be replaced by ramen noodles, which are found in Asian grocers and in supermarkets.

Preparation: 15 mins
Cooking: 10 mins

Serves 4

- 14 oz (400 g) fresh ramen noodles (or 9 oz/250 g dried ramen noodles)
- 1¾ oz (50 g) thin slices unsalted pork belly
- 1 cup (100 g) cabbage
- ¼ onion
- 1 tbsp neutral oil
- 1 tbsp fresh ginger, thinly sliced
- 1 tbsp soy sauce
- 2 tbsp oyster sauce

To garnish
- Pickled ginger
- ½ sheet nori, cut into thin strips

Tip
If you are using dried noodles, cook them in advance in a large quantity of water. There is no need to add water to the wok when you add them.

Preparation: 10 mins
Cooking: 3 mins

- 14 oz (400 g)
  somen noodles
- 1 scallion, green part
  only, finely chopped
- 2 tbsp sesame seeds
- 1 strip nori,
  finely chopped
- 1 small piece ginger,
  thinly sliced
- 2½ cups (600 ml) tsuyu
  sauce (see p. 27)

Hiyashi somen

Cook the somen noodles in a large saucepan of boiling water according to the instructions on the packet (2–3 minutes.)

Rinse the noodles under cold running water and drain. Arrange on a serving plate and sprinkle with sesame seeds.

Serve with the sauce on the side and the condiments in small dishes.

Somen are very thin wheat flour noodles, generally eaten cold in summer. They have a very quick cooking time, and must be rinsed under cold running water once cooked to halt the cooking process and avoid them sticking.

Tip
For a stronger flavor, add a little wasabi to the sauce.

Preparation: 20 mins
Cooking: 15 mins

- 14 oz (400 g) soba noodles
- 1 carrot
- 1¾ cups (400 g)
  fresh spinach
- 4 green asparagus stalks
- 1 tbsp toasted sesame oil
- 1 tbsp soy sauce
- 2½ cups (600 ml) miso soup
  (see p. 22)
- ⅔ cup (150 ml) sesame-
  flavored goma-dare sauce
  (see p. 26)
- 1 tbsp gomashio-
  (or sesame seeds)

Goma soba

Peel the carrot and cut into thin matchstick strips. Trim and wash the spinach. Clean the asparagus, remove the woody ends, and cut into 1 in- (3 cm-) lengths.

Heat the toasted sesame oil in a wok or skillet and fry the carrot and asparagus (except the tips) for 3–4 minutes.

Add the asparagus tips and cook all the vegetables for a further minute.

Add the spinach and cook for a further 3–4 minutes until wilted. Remove from the heat, season with soy sauce and set aside.

Cook the soba noodles in a large saucepan of boiling water according to the instructions on the packet (about 5 minutes.) Rinse under cold running water and drain.

Heat the miso soup in a saucepan, but do not let it boil.

Pour the sesame-flavored sauce into another saucepan, and water down with a little soup. Gradually pour in the remaining soup, as if making mayonnaise.

Divide the noodles between 4 bowls. Pour over sesame-flavored broth to cover and add the vegetables. Garnish with gomashio (or sesame seeds.)

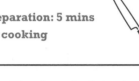

Preparation: 5 mins
No cooking

Makes 4 onigiri

- 2 bowls cooked rice (see Japanese rice p. 16)
- 2 umeboshi (pickled plums), pitted (available in organic stores and Asian grocers)
- ½ sheet nori seaweed, cut into 4 lengths
- salt

Onigiri

Onigiri with umeboshi

Sprinkle salt over your dampened hands. Scoop up a quarter of the rice and press it down compactly to form a triangle: the trick is to turn the triangle between your hands so as to maintain an even, light pressure on the three edges (without squashing the rice, which must on no account be crushed.)

Make a small depression in the center of the triangle and press half an umeboshi into the dip. Place 1 length of nori seaweed at the bottom of the onigiri.

Make 3 more onigiri with the remaining rice.

Variation: Onigiri with ham and peas

Gently mix 2 bowls of cooked rice (see Japanese rice on p. 16) with 1 shredded slice of ham, 2 tablespoons cooked peas, and a pinch of salt.

Dampen your hands then sprinkle with salt and make 4 triangles, following the instructions given opposite.

Onigiri (おにぎり) are snacks the Japanese enjoy at any time of day. These rice sandwiches are easy to carry around and are a practical way of using up last night's rice. Pickled plums (umeboshi) are most frequently used as a garnish, but this recipe could equally be served with other ingredients such as smoked fish or pickles.

Preparation: 5 mins
Cooking: 6 mins

Makes 4 onigiri

- 2 bowls cooked rice (see Japanese rice p. 16)
- ¼ can tuna in brine
- 3 tbsp flaked sea lettuce or nori (available in organic stores)
- 3 tbsp soy sauce
- salt

Broiled onigiri

Place the rice in a bowl. Add the drained and flaked tuna and the sea lettuce seaweed. Mix gently so as not to crush the rice grains.

Sprinkle salt over your dampened hands. Take up a quarter of the rice and press it down compactly to form a triangle: the trick is to turn the triangle between your hands so as to maintain an even, light pressure on the three edges (without squashing the rice, which must on no account be crushed.)

Make 3 more onigiri with the remaining rice.

Arrange the onigiri on a baking sheet lined with wax paper. Broil for about 2 minutes. Remove from the broiler and, using a brush, daub soy sauce over the onigiri; broil for 2 minutes; brush with soy sauce once more, turn over, and brush the other side with soy sauce; broil for a further 2 minutes.

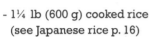

Preparation: 10 mins
Cooking: 12 mins

Serves 4

- 1¼ lb (600 g) cooked rice
  (see Japanese rice p. 16)
- 1½ tbsp vegetable oil
- 4 eggs
- Generous 1½ cups (180 g)
  fresh garden peas, shelled
- 2 scallions, finely chopped
- 1 tbsp fresh ginger, finely
  chopped
- 7 oz (200 g) small cooked
  shrimp
- 1 tbsp soy sauce
- 1 tbsp toasted sesame oil
- salt and freshly ground
  pepper

Yaki meshi

Beat the eggs with a pinch of salt in a bowl.

Heat 1 tablespoon of vegetable oil in a wok. Crack in the eggs and, as soon as they start to cook, mix with two chopsticks or a spatula. Take off the heat before the eggs are completely done. Transfer to a plate.

Wipe the wok, pour in the remaining vegetable oil, and cook the garden peas over medium heat for 3–4 minutes.

Add the scallions and ginger and cook for a further 2 minutes.

Add the shrimp then the cooked rice. Mix everything together over medium heat for 2–3 minutes. Season with soy sauce and toasted sesame oil.

Remove from the heat, add the scrambled eggs, and season with salt and pepper.

Serve immediately.

Preparation: 20 mins
Cooking: 10 mins

- 4 bowls white sushi rice (see p. 18)
- 2 eggs
- groundnut oil for frying
- 4 oz (120 g) very fresh salmon fillet
- 3½ oz (100 g) very fresh sea bream fillet
- 2 tbsp sesame seeds
- 4 shiso leaves (or a few arugula leaves)
- 2 tbsp flaked pickled ginger
- 1 strip nori, cut into thin strips
- wasabi
- soy sauce

Chirashi

Beat the eggs in a bowl.

Heat the oil in a nonstick skillet and pour in a little beaten egg to make a thin pancake. Cook for 1–2 minutes. Flip over the pancake and cook the other side for just a few seconds. Remove the pancake from the skillet and repeat the process until all the beaten egg is used up.

Stack the pancakes on a cutting board, roll up, and cut into thin circles.

Skin and bone the salmon and sea bream. Cut the fish into slices ⅓ in (1 cm) thick.

Divide the sushi rice between 4 bowls. Sprinkle with sesame seeds then arrange the pancake rounds, shiso leaves, salmon and sea bream slices, and the nori seaweed strips. Add a little wasabi and a few flakes of pickled ginger.

Mix a little soy sauce and wasabi in small dishes. Each diner will sprinkle sauce over his or her bowl of rice to taste before eating.

野菜 # Vegetables

Closely in tune with nature, Japan has developed a cuisine that follows the different seasons. Some vegetables, therefore, are only available on restaurant menus for a few days. Vegetables are often prepared in the simplest of ways, the better to appreciate their true flavor.

Dengaku eggplants

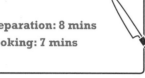

Serves 4

- 2 eggplants
- 2 tbsp red miso paste
- 1 tbsp sake
- 1 tbsp mirin
- 2 tbsp superfine sugar
- vegetable oil
- 2 tbsp sesame seeds
- 4 scallions, finely chopped

In a bowl, mix the miso paste, sake, mirin, and sugar till smooth.

Cut the eggplants in half lengthways. Score the flesh with the tip of a knife to create a lattice pattern.

Lay the eggplant halves face up on a baking sheet lined with wax paper. Broil for 3 minutes. Turn and drizzle over a little oil. Broil for a further 3 minutes, keeping a close eye on them all the time.

Spread the miso paste over the eggplant halves and sprinkle with sesame seeds. Place under the heat once again until caramelized (about 1 minute.)

Garnish with the finely chopped scallion and serve.

Tip
For a milder, sweeter flavor replace the red miso paste with white miso paste.

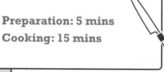

Serves 4

Preparation: 5 mins
Cooking: 15 mins

- 12 shiitake mushrooms
- 4½ oz (125 g) enoki
  (or button) mushrooms
- 4 ½ oz (125 g) shimeji
  (or oyster) mushrooms

For the sauce
- 2 tbsp soy sauce
- 2 tbsp toasted sesame oil
- 2 tbsp lemon juice

Mushroom parcels

Pre-heat the oven to 355 °F (Gas mark 4.)

Clean the mushrooms and cut off the stalks.

To make the sauce, pour the soy sauce, toasted
sesame oil, and lemon juice into a bowl. Mix well to
emulsify.

Divide the mushrooms between 4 pieces of wax
paper and pour over a little sauce. Draw up and
secure the little parcels with kitchen twine so they
look like candy.

Cook in the oven for 15 minutes.

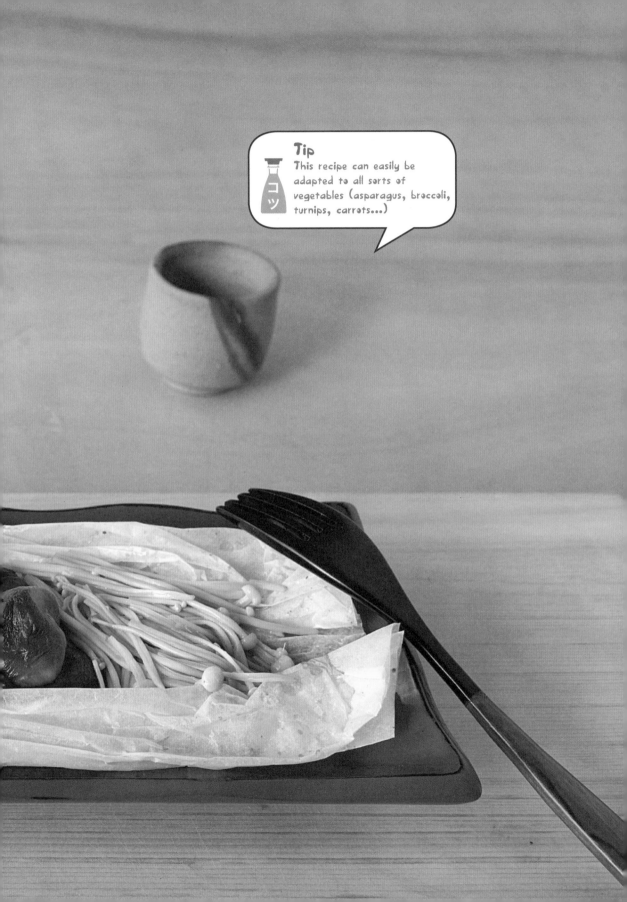

Preparation: 5 mins
Cooking: 1 min
Marinade : 30 mins

- 1¾ cups (400 g)
  fresh spinach
- pinch of salt
- 1 tbsp sesame seeds

For the sauce
- 6 tbsp dashi broth
  (see p. 20)
- 3 tbsp soy sauce
- 2 tbsp mirin

Ohitachi spinach

First, make the sauce, mixing the dashi broth, soy sauce, and mirin in a bowl.

Clean the spinach. Blanch for 1 minute in a large saucepan of salted boiling water and then plunge immediately in cold water. Drain and squeeze out excess water with your hands.

Arrange the spinach in a bowl. Pour over the sauce and marinate for at least 30 minutes.

Serve the spinach in a dish with the sauce and garnish with sesame seeds.

Mirin is an alcoholic sweetened rice beverage used exclusively in cooking and never as a drink. A few drops added to simmered vegetables, fish, or meat will sweeten the dish. Mirin is readily available from Asian grocers or supermarkets.

Green asparagus with ume sauce

Preparation: 5 mins
Cooking: 6 mins

- 1 bunch green asparagus
- 2 tbsp umeboshi paste
- 2 tbsp sake
- 1 tbsp mirin

Serves 4

Cut off the woody ends of the asparagus and peel if necessary. Cut in two lengthways.

Steam the asparagus for about 6 minutes.

To make the ume sauce, mix the umeboshi paste with the sake and mirin in a bowl.

Serve the asparagus with the ume sauce.

Umeboshi paste is lightly salted and fairly acid. It is made from Japanese plums (ume) that are marinated in red shiso leaves, which gives them their beautiful color. In Japan, umeboshi paste is frequently served in meals as an accompaniment to rice. It is readily available from Asian grocers or in organic stores.

- ⅔ cup (100 g) all-purpose flour
- ⅔ cup (100 g) rice flour
- 1 tsp salt

For the filling
- 1 tbsp vegetable oil
- 7 oz (200 g) carrots, peeled and cut into small dice
- 7 oz (200 g) green beans, trimmed and cut into small circles
- 3 level tbsp white miso paste
- 2 tbsp superfine sugar
- ½ tbsp toasted sesame oil

Oyaki

Sift both types of flour and the salt into a bowl. Combine with ½ cup (120 ml) of water and knead with your hands into a smooth and supple dough. Cover with a damp cloth and leave to rest for 15 minutes.

Divide the dough into 8 pieces. Roll out each piece into a circle about 3 in (8 cm) in diameter.

To make the filling, heat the vegetable oil in a skillet and fry the vegetables for about 3 minutes. Add 7 tbsp (100 ml) of water. Cover, lower the heat, and cook until the water has been absorbed.

Mix the miso paste and the sugar in a bowl. Add this mixture to the vegetables and cook for a further 2 minutes.

To make the oyaki, place 2 tablespoons of filling on each dough circle. Bring the sides of the dough up over the filling to form a pocket and pinch the edges at the top to seal (remove any excess dough.)

Heat the toasted sesame oil in a skillet and brown the oyaki on both sides, flattening them gently with a spatula. Pour on water to come halfway up the sides of the skillet, cover, and cook over high heat until the water has been totally absorbed.

Remove the lid and cook the oyaki for a further 2 minutes on each side. Serve immediately.

魚と甲殻類

Fish and shellfish

Entirely surrounded by water, Japan has developed a cuisine that relies heavily on produce from the sea: fish, shellfish, and even dried seaweed—you can really taste the sea in many of the dishes. Japanese cuisine is renowned for its raw fish, of course, but this chapter also includes other easy recipes for fish that will open up new culinary horizons for you!

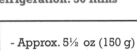

Serves 4

- Approx. 5½ oz (150 g)
  sea bream fillet
- 1 avocado
- 2 sheets shiso (or 2 sprigs
  cilantro)
- 2 tbsp lemon juice
- 2 tbsp soy sauce

Sea bream tartare

Skin and bone the sea bream; cut it into small dice.

Peel the avocado, remove the pit, and cut into small dice.

Finely chop the sheets of shiso.

Carefully mix the fish, avocado, and shiso in a bowl. Season with soy sauce and lemon juice. Refrigerate for 30 minutes.

Shiso (or perilla) is very fragrant and is ideal to accompany raw fish or salads. This herb belongs to the mint family, but its delicate flavor is much more subtle. It is frequently found in Asian grocers' stores under its Vietnamese name of "tito". Cilantro or arugula are good alternatives.

Tip
You can use a fish of your choice instead for this tartare (sardines, anchovies, salmon...)

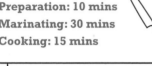

VG

Salmon teriyaki

Preparation: 10 mins
Marinating: 30 mins
Cooking: 15 mins

Serves 4

- 4 salmon steaks, approx. 5½ oz (150 g) each
- 7 tbsp (100 ml) teriyaki sauce (see p. 27)
- 2 tsp fresh ginger, grated
- 1 handful snow peas
- 1 handful bean sprouts
- 2 tbsp sesame seeds

Skin and bone the salmon.

Mix the teriyaki sauce and the ginger in a bowl. Marinate the salmon steaks in this sauce for 30 minutes in the refrigerator.

Steam the snow peas and bean sprouts for about 5 minutes.

Heat a nonstick skillet. Drain the salmon—reserving the marinade—and seal over medium heat for 3–4 minutes on each side. Set aside on a plate.

Wipe dry the skillet with paper towels. Pour the marinade into the skillet, return to the heat, and allow the marinade to reduce for 2–3 minutes, until it caramelizes.

Put the salmon back in the skillet and carefully coat each steak in the hot sauce.

Arrange the salmon and vegetables on a serving plate and garnish with sesame seeds.

Preparation: 20 mins
Cooking: 10 mins

For the tempura batter
- 1 egg yolk
- ⅔ cup (100 g) all-
  purpose flour, sifted
- ½ tsp baking soda
- ¾ cup (200 ml) ice water

For the garnish
- 8 large shrimp
- 8 shiitake mushrooms
- 12 okra pods (or 1 small
  head broccoli)
- oil for frying
- ¼ daikon, peeled
  and grated
- 4 sheets shiso seaweed
  (optional)
- tsuyu (see p. 27)

Shrimp tempura

Mix the tempura batter ingredients in a bowl until thoroughly smooth.

Remove the stalks from the shiitake mushrooms and trim off the ends of the okra.

Peel the shrimp, leaving the tail intact; cut along the back, and remove the black vein with the tip of a knife.

Heat the frying oil to about 340 °F (170 °C.) Drop a piece of bread into the oil: if it starts to bubble, the oil is heated to a sufficiently high temperature.

Dip the shrimp, mushrooms, and okra in the tempura batter then drop the battered vegetables immediately in the frying oil (work in several batches.) Deep fry until pale golden in color. Drain on paper towels.

Arrange the tempura fritters on a serving plate with the sheets of shiso and a little grated daikon.

To eat, dip the fritters in the tsuyu sauce, flavored with some grated daikon.

Marinated fish with miso

To make the marinade, mix all the ingredients in a dish that has a lid.

Place the swordfish slices in the marinade, taking care to coat them thoroughly in the marinade. Put the lid on the dish and allow to marinate for 1–3 days in the refrigerator.

On the day you wish to serve the fish, pre-heat the oven to 400 °F (200 °C.) Take the fish out of the dish and drain off the excess marinade.

Place the fish on a baking sheet lined with wax paper.

Bake for 8–10 minutes, depending on the thickness of the fish. Finish off the cooking by broiling for 1 minute.

Arrange the swordfish slices on a serving plate with the pickled ginger.

Preparation: 10 mins
Marinating: 1–3 days
Cooking: 10 mins

- 2 slices swordfish
- few slivers pickled ginger

For the marinade
- 3½ oz (100 g) white miso paste
- 4 tbsp mirin
- 4 tbsp sake
- 2 tbsp superfine sugar

Serves 4

Steamed sea bass with ponzu sauce

Preparation: 10 mins
Cooking: 15 mins

- 4 sea bass, approx. 9 oz (250 g), scaled and cleaned
- 2 leeks
- ⅔ cup (150 ml) ponzu sauce (see p. 26)
- 3 tbsp toasted sesame oil

Cut away the hard green part of the leeks. Cut them into thin matchstick strips.

Place the leek strips in an electric steamer and lay the sea bass on top. Cover and cook for 12–15 minutes.

Arrange the sea bass and leeks on a serving plate. Sprinkle with a little ponzu sauce.

Heat the toasted sesame oil in a large saucepan until smoking. Pour it at once over the fish and serve immediately.

Tip
Check that the fish is done by inserting a wooden skewer in its thickest part (it should go in easily.)

Serves 6

Preparation: 5 mins
Cooking: 15 mins
Standing: 10 mins

- head and carcass of
  1 large sea bream
- scant 2½ cups (480 g)
  white rice
- 1 sheet kombu, 4 in
  (10 cm) long
- 1 dried shiitake
  mushroom
- 3 tbsp soy sauce
- 3 tbsp mirin
- few chives,
  finely chopped
- pinch of salt

Tai meshi

Rinse the rice in several changes of water until the water runs clear. Drain and transfer to a large saucepan with 2½ cups (600 ml) water.

Add the kombu seaweed and shiitake mushroom to the saucepan, then lay the carcass and head of the sea bream on top. Season with soy sauce, mirin, and salt. Cover and bring to a boil then cook over very low heat for 12 minutes.

Remove the saucepan from the heat and stand, covered, for about 10 minutes.

Take off any pieces of sea bream flesh from around the carcass—as well as the cheeks—and arrange them on a plate. Remove the head, carcass, kombu seaweed, and shiitake mushroom from the saucepan.

Gently stir the sea bream flesh and cheeks into the rice.

Divide between bowls and garnish with the finely chopped chives.

This recipe is very simple. It is often made with a whole sea bream, but it can also, as I suggest here, be made with just the carcass. Ask your fish merchant to cut off fillets to eat in, say, sashimi. This will enable you to make two dishes with the same fish!

Preparation: 10 mins
No cooking

Serves 8

- 1 salmon fillet
- 1 sea bream fillet
- 1 scorpion fish fillet
- 1 mackerel fillet
- 8 scallops
- 8 sheets shiso (optional)
- 1 small piece daikon,
  peeled (optional)
- few slivers pickled ginger

To serve
- soy sauce
- wasabi

Sashimi selection

Skin and bone the fish, taking care to remove all the dark parts sticking to the flesh.

Cut the fish fillets into ¼-inch- (½-cm-) thick slices.

Cut the scallops into 2 or 3 strips widthways (depending on their size.)

Arrange the fish slices and scallop strips on a serving platter. Garnish with shiso seaweed sheets, daikon cut into thin strips, and pickled ginger.

To serve the raw fish, dip in soy sauce flavored with a dash of wasabi. Accompany with a bowl of rice (see 'Japanese rice' on p.16.)

Sashimi is like sushi, but without the small rice ball. For best results—it goes without saying that—only the best-quality fish should be used. To be sure of its freshness ask your fish merchant!

Preparation: 10 mins
Cooking: few seconds

- 2¼ lb (1 kg) salmon fillet
- 3 tbsp soy sauce
- 1 tbsp rice vinegar
- 1 tsp fresh ginger, grated
- 1 tbsp sesame seeds

Variation: Salmon tataki

Heat a skillet over high heat and sear the salmon for a few seconds on each side. Take the fish out of the skillet and cut it into strips ¼ inch (½ cm) thick. Arrange on a serving platter.

To make the seasoning, mix the soy sauce, rice vinegar, and ginger. Pour over the salmon strips and garnish with sesame seeds.

Tataki is the name given to fish (or beef) that is briefly seared then cut into slices the same way as sashimi. It is usually seasoned before serving. Even if the fish remains raw in the center, its flavor is totally different. It is—quite simply—succulent!

Tip

To obtain fish slices that are sufficiently large (with fish that are not very thick, such as sea bream), cut the fillets so they are almost parallel to the cutting board—do not cut them vertically.

Sashimi selection

肉 Meat

Meat is also eaten in Japan—albeit in small quantities—and yakitori skewers have become as well known as sushi. Try a few essential dishes from Japanese culinary culture, such as the very convivial shabu-shabu or the flavorful tonkatsu.

Preparation: 10 mins
Cooking: 10 mins

- 1 chicken thigh
- 2 scallions
- generous ¾ cup (200 ml) dashi broth (see p. 20)
- 4 tbsp soy sauce
- 4 tbsp mirin
- 4 eggs
- 4 bowls cooked white rice (see p. 16)
- ½ sheet nori, cut into thin strips

Oyako-don

Bone the chicken, remove the skin, and cut the flesh into strips.

Finely chop the scallions (reserving a little green part for the garnish.)

Bring the dashi broth to a boil in a wok. Add the chicken strips, scallions, soy sauce, and mirin. Cook over medium heat for about 5 minutes.

In a bowl, stir the eggs without beating them and pour them into the wok, stirring gently. Cook until the eggs have set.

Divide the cooked rice between bowls. Pour the mixture over the rice, then garnish with the green part of the scallions and the nori seaweed strips.

This dish, which is very popular in Japan, is a donburi, or a garnish served in a bowl of rice. Okayo means literally "parents and children."

Tip
If you ask your butcher to bone the chicken thigh for you, it will save you time!

Shabu-shabu

Preparation: 15 mins
Soaking: 30 mins
Cooking: at table,
during the meal

Serves 4

- generous 1 lb (500 g)
  beef fillet
- 1 piece kombu seaweed,
  4 in (20 cm)
- 1 carrot
- 2 leeks
- ¼ Chinese cabbage
- 8 shiitake (or button)
  mushrooms
- 14 oz (400 g) firm tofu
- 1¼ cups (300 ml) gome-
  dare (see p. 26)

Pour 2 quarts (2 liters) of water into a large saucepan, add the kombu seaweed, and leave to infuse for at least 30 minutes.

Meanwhile, peel the carrot and cut it into rounds. Cut the leeks into lengths. Cut the Chinese cabbage into 1½-inch- (4-cm-) chunks. Trim the stalks from the mushrooms. Drain the tofu and cut into cubes of about 1½ inches (4 cm.)

Cut the beef fillet into very thin slices with a very sharp knife.

Arrange the vegetables, tofu, and meat on a large serving platter.

Pour the kombu seaweed broth into a large saucepan. Place it in the center of the table on a portable stove and bring to a boil. Remove the kombu seaweed.

When you are ready to sit down and eat, drop the vegetables one by one into the broth. Then, each diner takes turns to poach slices of meat and tofu in the broth. Meat, vegetables, and tofu can all be eaten together, dipped in the gome-dare served in a small bowl.

Tip
At the end of the meal you can enjoy the broth, which will have absorbed all the different flavors of the dish.

Yakitori selection

Preparation: 15 mins
Cooking: 15 mins

- 2 chicken thighs
- 16 shiitake (or button) mushrooms
- 3 long leeks (preferably thin)
- generous ¾ cup (200 ml) yakitori sauce (see p. 26)

Bone the chicken thighs, remove the skin, and cut the flesh into cubes. Thread on to 8 wooden skewers.

Remove the stalks from the mushrooms. Thread 2 mushrooms on to 8 wooden skewers.

Cut the leeks into 1½-inch- (4-cm-) lengths. Steam for 5 minutes and thread on to 8 wooden skewers.

Line a baking sheet with wax paper. Make two cylinders out of aluminum foil and arrange them on the baking sheet leaving a space between them. Place the skewers between the aluminum foil cylinders so the ends are supported and taking care that that nothing touches the bottom of the baking sheet.

Broil the skewers until they begin to color lightly. Remove from the heat and dip them in a little yakitori sauce. Turn them and broil the other side for a further 2–3 minutes.

Continue to broil a further 3–4 times, dipping them in a little yakitori sauce and turning them each time, until cooked through.

Tip
Your wooden skewers will not burn under the broiler if you soak them in cold water for **30** minutes before threading the ingredients on to them.

Yakitori selection

Serves 4

Preparation: 15 mins
Cooking: 10 mins

- 12 thin slices unsalted
  pork belly
- 3½ oz (100 g) green beans
- 4 green asparagus
- 4 okra pods
- 1 handful arugula
- 4 tsp umeboshi paste
- 2 tbsp mirin

Niku maki

Trim the green beans. Remove the stalk from the okra.

Remove the woody ends of the asparagus and peel them if necessary. Cut them into 2–3 sections, depending on their size. Steam the asparagus for 5 minutes with the green beans and the okra.

To make the rolls, arrange a few leaves of arugula, some green beans, and a little umeboshi paste on a slice of pork. Roll up to close the niku maki. Make another 3 niku maki in the same way.

Make 4 more rolls using asparagus as the main filling ingredient and 4 more rolls using okra as the main ingredient.

Place the rolls in a skillet and brown them over medium heat on all sides for 4–5 minutes.

Add the mirin and cook for a further 1 minute, turning the niku maki all the time. Serve very hot.

Tonkatsu

Preparation: 10 mins
Cooking: 10 mins

Shred the cabbage. Beat the egg in a dish. Pour the flour and breadcrumbs into two other dishes.

Season the pork scallops with salt and pepper. Dip them in the flour then in the beaten egg, and finally in the breadcrumbs (taking care that the breadcrumbs stick well.)

Heat the oil in a wok (drop a small piece of bread in the oil: if bubbles appear around it, it has reached the right temperature.) Cook the scallops for about 5 minutes until golden (in 2 batches). Drain on paper towels.

Cut the scallops into slices and arrange on a bed of shredded cabbage on a serving platter.

Coat with tonkatsu sauce and add the lemon wedges. Serve accompanied with a bowl of rice.

Serves 4

- 4 pork scallops, approx. 5½ oz (150 g) each
- 14 oz (400 g) green cabbage
- 1 egg
- 4 tbsp all-purpose flour
- 4–6 tbsp "Panko" breadcrumbs (available from Asian grocers) or ordinary breadcrumbs
- oil for frying
- 7 tbsp (100 ml) tonkatsu sauce (see p. 27)
- ½ lemon, quartered
- 4 bowls cooked white rice (see p. 16)
- salt and pepper

Tip
If you are short of time, store-bought tonkatsu sauce is available from Asian grocers.

コツ

卵と豆腐

Eggs
and tofu

Tofu—known also as "vegetarian steak"—is a soy-based food which is high in protein. It also has the advantage of being fairly bland and therefore will soak up all the different flavors in a dish (salty, acid, spicy, bitter, sweet.) I would like to share some recipes with you that will take you on a voyage of discovery into tofu and what it can offer.

Preparation: 5 mins
Cooking: 25 mins

- 3 eggs
- 1⅔ cups (400 ml) dashi broth
  (see p. 20)
- ½ tbsp soy sauce
- 2 tbsp mirin
- 1 tsp salt
- 2 oz (60 g) small raw shrimp,
  deveined
- 12 snow peas

Chawan mushi

Pre-heat the oven to 300 °F (150 °C.)

Beat the eggs and dashi broth together in a bowl.
Add the soy sauce, mirin, and salt.

Divide the shrimp and snow peas between
4 ramekins (reserving a few shrimps and peas for
the garnish.) Pour over the egg mixture.

Cover the ramekins with aluminum foil and place
on a rack over an oven pan. Pour 2 glasses of water
into the bottom of the pan. Place in the oven and
cook for 20 minutes. Arrange the reserved shrimp
and snow peas on top of the ramekins and cook for
a further 5 minutes.

Tip
You can also cook the chawan
mushi in an electric steamer,
in which case you will not need
to cover the ramekins with
aluminum foil.

Hiyashi tofu

Preparation: 10 mins
No cooking

Cut the tofu into 12 cubes.

Cut the tomato into thin dice.

Sprinkle the grated ginger and scallion over
4 tofu cubes.

Sprinkle the tomato dice and sesame seeds over
4 of the other tofu cubes.

Arrange a little wasabi on the remaining tofu cubes.

Put 1 of each sort of tofu cube on each plate.
Sprinkle the tomato ones with toasted sesame oil.

Serve with soy sauce.

*The two main varieties of tofu are firm and silken. The
latter is creamier and usually served on its own with a
little soy sauce. To keep tofu once it is opened, put it in a
container and cover it with cold water. It can be stored like
this for 4 days in the refrigerator. Just remember to change
the water every day.*

- 14 oz (400 g) silken tofu,
  drained
- ½ tomato
- 2 tsp fresh ginger, grated
- 2 scallions,
  finely chopped
- 2 tsp sesame seeds
- 1 tsp wasabi
- 1 tbsp toasted sesame oil

Serves 4

Preparation: 10 mins
Cooking: 10 mins

- 6 eggs
- 7 tbsp (100 ml) dashi broth (see p. 20)
- 2 tsp soy sauce
- 2 tbsp mirin
- vegetable oil for frying
- 3 tbsp cooked and finely chopped spinach

To serve
- grated daikon
- soy sauce

Tamagoyaki with spinach

Beat the eggs with the dashi broth, soy sauce, and mirin in a bowl.

Heat 1 tbsp vegetable oil in a skillet then pour in a small amount of beaten egg to make a thin pancake.

Arrange the spinach in a line across the pancake, lift up the edge closest to you and fold over to cover the spinach.

Roll up the pancake until you reach the opposite side of the skillet.

Grease the skillet if necessary with oiled paper towels.

Once again, pour a small amount of beaten egg mixture into the skillet. Lift the rolled-up pancake slightly to let a little beaten egg run underneath.

Cook until set, then roll up the new pancake until you reach the opposite side of the skillet.

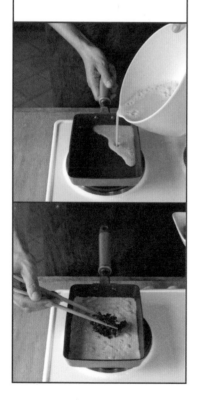

Repeat the process until you have used up all the beaten egg mixture. You will obtain a rectangular or cylindrical omelet depending on the shape of the skillet.

Lightly brown the omelet on all sides over medium heat.

Place the omelet in the center of a maki rolling mat on a work surface. Fold the edges of the mat over the omelet to cover it and press down well to make a block.

Cut the omelet into slices and serve with a little grated daikon and soy sauce.

This delicious Japanese-style omelet is created by rolling up thin egg pancakes one after the other. It can be served with rice or as sushi.

Tip
For a change, try replacing the spinach with another vegetable such as green beans, or use flaked crabmeat.

Tamagoyaki with spinach

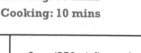

Serves 4

- 9 oz (250 g) firm tofu, drained
- 2 dried shiitake mushrooms
- 1 carrot, peeled and grated
- 1 egg
- ½ tbsp fresh ginger, grated
- 2 tbsp potato flour
- 1 tbsp soy sauce
- 1 tsp salt
- oil for frying

Tofu burgers

Wrap the tofu in paper towels and place between two cutting boards to drain for 15 minutes.

Soak the shiitake mushrooms for about 10 minutes in a small saucepan containing 1 glass of water, to rehydrate them.

Bring the saucepan to a boil. Remove from the heat and infuse for 10 minutes.

Drain the shiitake mushrooms (you can reserve the soaking liquid, which will make good broth), remove the stalks, and chop finely. Pat dry with paper towels.

In a bowl, mash the tofu with a fork. Add the carrot, mushrooms, the egg, ginger, potato flour, soy sauce, and salt. Mix well, then shape into 8 small balls.

Heat the oil in a wok then drop in the balls, in several batches. Brown each batch for about 5 minutes, then drain on paper towels.

Serves 4

- 11 oz (300 g) firm tofu, drained
- 1 clove garlic, green shoot removed, finely chopped
- 2 tbsp all-purpose flour
- 2 tbsp toasted sesame oil
- 1 handful bean sprouts
- 7 tbsp (100 ml) ponzu sauce (see p. 26)
- 4 scallions, finely chopped
- salt and freshly ground pepper

Tofu steak

Wrap the tofu in paper towels and press between two cutting boards to drain for 15 minutes.

Remove the paper towels and cut the tofu into 4 slices. Season with salt and pepper on each side. Sprinkle with garlic and coat lightly in flour.

Heat 1 tbsp toasted sesame oil in a skillet and stir-fry the bean sprouts over high heat for 2–3 minutes. Set aside on a plate.

Pour the remaining oil into the skillet and brown the tofu slices over medium heat for 3 minutes on each side.

Arrange 1 slice of browned tofu and a few bean sprouts on each plate. Sprinkle with ponzu sauce and garnish with scallion.

Tofu sukiyaki

To make the sukiyaki sauce, put all the ingredients for the sauce in a saucepan and bring to a boil. Stir to dissolve the sugar. Set aside.

Heat the oil in a large saucepan and add the tofu cubes, leeks, shiitake mushrooms, and thinly sliced cabbage. Sprinkle over a little sukiyaki sauce and simmer for 5–6 minutes, until the leeks are tender.

Add the spinach. As soon as it starts to wilt, remove from the heat. Sprinkle with scallion.

To serve, each diner breaks and lightly beats 1 egg in a bowl. During the course of the meal, the diner uses the beaten egg as a dip for the cubes of tofu and vegetables, as required.

Serves 4

- 14 oz (400 g) firm tofu, drained and cubed
- ½ tbsp vegetable oil
- 2 leeks, cut into lengths
- 4 shiitake mushrooms, halved
- ¼ Chinese cabbage, thinly sliced
- 1 cup (200 g) spinach
- 1 scallion, green part only, thinly sliced
- 4 fresh organic eggs

For the sukiyaki sauce
- 6 tbsp soy sauce
- 6 tbsp mirin
- 3 tbsp sake
- 3 tbsp water
- 3 tbsp superfine sugar

Tip
This traditional dish is usually made with slices of beef. Here is a vegetarian version which will make you truly appreciate tofu. To complete the dish, serve with a bowl of rice.

Desserts

デザート

In Japan, desserts are often just a piece of fruit. Japanese sweet things—in particular those based on sweet red bean paste (anko)—are traditionally eaten on their own, with green tea, and not as part of a meal. French patisserie, however, has had an influence and nowadays desserts—with a Japanese twist—are more fashionable. Highly original desserts flavored with matcha (green tea) powder, sesame, or yuzu (a Japanese citrus fruit) have been invented.

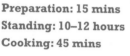

Preparation: 15 mins
Standing: 10–12 hours
Cooking: 45 mins

Sesame seed cheesecake

For the base
- 4½ oz (125 g) plain cookies
- 3½ tbsp (50 g) butter, melted
- small pinch salt
- ¼ oz (35 g) black sesame seeds

For the filling
- 1¼ lb (600 g) cottage cheese
- ⅔ cup (150 ml) crème fraîche
- 9 tbsp (125 g) cane sugar
- 2 eggs
- black sesame seeds

To make the base, grind the cookies to a powder in a mixer. Add the melted butter, salt, and sesame seeds and mix again.

Spread out the cookie mixture in a high-sided pan. Pat down lightly with the back of a spoon to flatten. Refrigerate for 30 minutes until the piecrust has firmed up slightly.

Pre-heat the oven to 355 °F (180 °C.)

To make the filling, beat the cottage cheese and sour cream in a bowl until very smooth. Add the sugar and eggs and beat again until the mixture is creamy.

Pour the filling over the prepared base, smoothing it with a spatula. Bake for 45 minutes.

Cool the cheesecake to room temperature, then store in the refrigerator for 10–12 hours before eating. Sprinkle with sesame seeds just before serving.

Tip
The black sesame seeds can be replaced by ordinary ivory-colored sesame seeds. The flavor will be different but the cheesecake will be equally good!

コツ

Preparation: 10 mins
Cooking: 2 mins
Standing: 1 hour

- 4 tangerines
- 7 tbsp (100 ml) water
- 1 tbsp agave syrup
  (available from organic
  stores) or cane syrup
- ½ tsp agar

Tangerine jelly dessert with agar

Cut the tops off the tangerines and, with a spoon, gently remove the whole fruit, taking care to preserve the peel shell in one piece. Put the shells to one side.

Purée the tangerine flesh in a food processor. Press through a strainer, trying to extract as much of the pulp as possible.

Pour the water, agave syrup, and agar powder into a small saucepan and stir. Bring to a boil and simmer for 30 seconds. Remove the saucepan from the heat and add the tangerine juice, stirring continuously.

Pour the jelly mixture into the tangerine shells, cool, and refrigerate for 1 hour.

Tip
Agar is a powerful gelling agent which has to be carefully controlled. Take care not to use too much or your jelly dessert will be too firm.

コツ

Serves 4

Preparation: 10 mins
Cooking: 2 mins
Standing: overnight

- 3½ oz (100 g) semisweet chocolate
- 10 oz (280 g) silken tofu
- 2 tbsp agave syrup (available from organic stores) or cane syrup
- scant 1 tsp matcha or hazelnut powder (optional)

Choco-tofu mousse

The day before, break the chocolate into pieces and melt in a saucepan with 2 tablespoons of water over very low heat.

Remove the saucepan from the heat as soon as the squares begin to soften and leave the chocolate to continue to melt.

Add the tofu (cut into chunks) and the agave syrup. Stir well to obtain a mousse-like texture. Refrigerate overnight.

The following day, sprinkle matcha or hazelnut powder over the mousse.

Tip
Instead of sprinkling matcha powder over the finished dessert, it can be incorporated in the mousse during the preparation. Chocolate goes very well with matcha.

Chestnut yokan

Preparation: 5 mins
Cooking: 2 mins
Refrigeration: 1 hour

- ⅔ cup (150 ml) water
- 1 tsp agar
- 6½ oz (180 g) sweetened chestnut paste
- few marrons glacés (for the decoration)

Serves 4

Stir the water and the agar powder together in a saucepan. Bring to a boil and simmer for 30 seconds.

Remove from the heat, add the chestnut paste, and whip until smooth.

Pour the mixture into a 5 x 4-inch- (12 x 10-cm-) mold and cool. Refrigerate for at least 1 hour before serving, cut into rectangular pieces, and garnish with chopped up marrons glacés.

Agar (or kanten, in Japanese) is a natural gelling agent derived from a type of red seaweed. It is an excellent substitute for gelatin because it is healthier. It needs to be boiled for a few seconds to develop its gelling qualities. Agar is sold in most organic stores.

Matcha, almond, and lemon tart

Preparation: 15 mins
Cooking: 25 mins

For 1 tart, 10 in (26 cm) dia., or 6 tartlets
- 9 oz (250 g) pastry
- 1 tsp matcha powder

For the almond and matcha filling
- scant 3 tsp matcha powder
- 2 tbsp almond paste
- 1½ oz (40 g) almond powder
- 2 tbsp agave syrup

For the lemon cream
- juice of 1 lemon
- 6 tbsp (80 g) superfine sugar
- 4 eggs, beaten
- 1 tbsp cornstarch

Pre-heat the oven to 355 °F (180 °C.)

Line a tart pan with the pastry. Bake for 12 minutes.

To make the almond and matcha filling, dilute the matcha powder in 3 tablespoons of hot water in a bowl. Add the remaining almond and matcha filling ingredients and mix together.

Take out of the oven and spread the almond and matcha filling inside the tart base with a spatula. Bake for a further 6 minutes. Cool.

To make the lemon cream, mix the lemon juice, sugar, eggs, and cornstarch in a saucepan. Cook over low heat, stirring frequently with a spatula, until the mixture begins to thicken. Immediately remove the saucepan from the heat, whipping continuously.

Spread the lemon cream over the almond and matcha filling. Smooth it out carefully and allow to cool. Sprinkle with matcha powder before serving.

© Cyril Castaing

Metric	American measure	Imperial
5 ml	1 tsp	1 tsp
15 ml	1 tbsp	1 tbsp
35 ml	2 ½ tbsp	2 ½ tbsp
65 ml	¼ cup	2 fl oz
125 ml	½ cup	4 ½ fl oz
250 ml	1 cup	9 fl oz
500 ml	2 cups	17 fl oz
1 liter	4 cups	1 quart

Metric	American measure	Imperial
30 g	1 oz	1 oz
55 g	2 oz	2 oz
115 g	4 oz	4 oz
170 g	6 oz	6 oz
225 g	8 oz	8 oz
454 g	1 lb (16 oz)	1 lb

Temperature	°Celsius	° Fahrenheit	Gas mark
Very cool	140 °C	275 °F	1
Cool	150 °C	300 °F	2
Warm moderate	160 °C	325 °F	3
	180 °C	350 °F	4
Fairly hot Hot	190–200 °C	375–400 °F	5–6
	220 °C	425 °F	7
Very hot	230–240 °C	450–475 °F	8–9

Conversions

さようなら。
Sayonara! *

どうもありがとう
Dõmo arigato! **

A big thank you to all those who helped to create this amazing project, particularly to Patrice, without whose help nothing would have been possible, and to the warm and friendly team at Mango, who allowed me the honor of coming to Gigors to taste some of their Japanese specialties!

* See you again! ** Thank you very much!

The following addresses can be useful for Japanese food and cooking utensils:

UK-based online shops:
http://www.japancentre.com/
http://www.japanesekitchen.co.uk/

US-based online shops:
http://www.marukaiestore.com/
http://store.mitsuwa.com/storefront.aspx
http://www.japansuper.com/

It is advisable not to serve dishes that contain raw eggs to very young children, pregnant women, elderly people, or to anyone weakened by serious illness. If in any doubt, consult your doctor. Be sure that all the eggs you use are as fresh as possible.

© Mango, Paris – 2012
Original Title: *Cuisine japonaise : les bases*
Original ISBN: 978-23-17003-57-8

Editorial Directors: Barbara Sabatier and Aurélie Cazenave
Graphic Design: Laurent Quellet
Photoengraving: Amalthéa
Production: Thierry Dubus et Marie Guibert

© for this English edition: h.f.ullmann publishing GmbH

Translation from French: Anna Bennett in association with First Edition Translations Ltd, Cambridge, UK
Typesetting: The Write Idea in association with First Edition Translations Ltd, Cambridge, UK

Project management for h.f.ullmann: Lars Pietzschmann

Overall responsibility for production: h.f.ullmann publishing GmbH, Potsdam, Germany

Printed in India, 2015

ISBN 978-3-8480-0754-7

10 9 8 7 6 5 4 3 2 1
X IX VIII VII VI V IV III II I

www.ullmann-publishing.com
newsletter@ullmann-publishing.com
facebook.com/ullmann.social